Without an Alibi

PHILIP NEILSEN is a poet, fiction writer and editor living in Brisbane, Australia, where he is Professor of English and Creative Writing at the Queensland University of Technology. His short stories have been widely anthologised and he also has written award winning fiction for young adults and children, translated into several languages. He is the editor of *Dotlit*, an on-line journal of creative writing based at QUT. *Without an Alibi* is his fifth collection of poetry.

Also by Philip Neilsen

Poetry
 Faces of a Sitting Man
 The Art of Lying
 Life Movies
 We'll All Go Together (with Barry O'Donohue)

Other Books
 Imagined Lives: a study of David Malouf
 Emma and the Megahero
 The Lie
 The Wombat King
 Edward Britton (with Gary Crew)

Editor
 The Penguin Book of Australian Satirical Verse
 The Sting in the Wattle

Without an Alibi

PHILIP NEILSEN

SALT

CAMBRIDGE

PUBLISHED BY SALT PUBLISHING
PO Box 937, Great Wilbraham, Cambridge CB21 5JX United Kingdom

All rights reserved

© Philip Neilsen, 2008

The right of Philip Neilsen to be identified as the
author of this work has been asserted by him in accordance
with Section 77 of the Copyright, Designs and Patents Act 1988.

This book is in copyright. Subject to statutory exception
and to provisions of relevant collective licensing agreements,
no reproduction of any part may take place without the written
permission of Salt Publishing.

First published 2008

Printed and bound in the United Kingdom by Biddles Ltd, Kings Lynn, Norfolk

Typeset in Swift 9.5 / 13

*This book is sold subject to the conditions that it shall not,
by way of trade or otherwise, be lent, re-sold, hired out,
or otherwise circulated without the publisher's prior consent
in any form of binding or cover other than that in which
it is published and without a similar condition including this
condition being imposed on the subsequent purchaser.*

ISBN 978 1 84471 286 1 hardback

Salt Publishing Ltd gratefully acknowledges
the financial assistance of Arts Council England

1 3 5 7 9 8 6 4 2

To my wife
Mhairead MacLeod

Contents

I **THE FOREST**   1
   Narrative of a Leaf   3
   Literary Forests   4
   The Black Forest   10
   The Conservative Forest   13
   The Imperial Forest   14
   St Martin and St Boniface Destroy the Forest Gods   16
   Sigurd is Instructed by the Birds   19
   Brynhildr Becomes a Nature Goddess   21
   Brisbane, 1959–1960   23
   Clouds   25
   Crusoe Revisited   26
   Death will be Unsighted   28
   Statues   29
   Northern Hairy-Nosed Wombat   30
   Gangway   31
   In Praise of Bears   32
   Jim Corbett Has the Idea for a National Park   33
   Koreelah Ranges, Northern NSW   36
   Ecological Love Poem   38
   May Gibbs in the New Suburbs   39
   Plantation—Glasshouse Mountains   40
   Anatomy of a Forest   41
   Public Liability   43
   Recording the Birds   45
   Salt   47
   The Art of Memory   49
   The Lost Valley   51

	The Fairy-Tale Forest	56
	The Man Who Couldn't See Colours	57
	The Need for Seclusion	60
	Fontainbleau Forest	62
	Bedtime Story	63
	Tree-planting	64
	Under the Cover of Shared Pleasures	65
	Wilderness	66
	Carbon Dioxide	67
	Bush Lullaby 2	68
II	METAMORPHOSIS	69
	The Anteater	71
	Walking with Shoulder Bags	72
	Suburban Dinner (1)	74
	The Investigation (2)	75
	Taking Off from Cyprus	76
	Tavistock Square July 7, 2005	78
	First Creative Writing Class	79
	Do We Have to Read the Set Books?	80
	Six Curses	81
	After I Died	82
	Poetry at Hanging Rock	84
	The Lie of Biology	86
	The Romance of the Clockmakers	88
	Workplace Bullying	90
	Biggles Flies Again at 95	91
	Harry Potter Book 8	92
	Roy Orbison in Germany	94
	Academic Party	95
	In Search of Shakespeare	96

Practising Blues Piano Scales	98
Lewis Carroll's Counsellor	99
George Bush in Brisbane	100
Breaking Up	101
Pets	102
Les A. Murray versus John Tranter at the Sydney Cricket Ground	103
Blaming Your Childhood	106
Hold the Grave Close	107
Metamorphosis	108

Acknowledgements

Some of the poems in this collection have previously appeared in *Agenda (UK)*, *China's Australia: a poetic anthology* ed. Ouyang Yu, *Southerly*, *The Courier Mail*, *Synaptic Graffiti*, *Fifty Years of Queensland Poetry* (CQUP), *The Sting in the Wattle* (UQP), *Overland* and *Wet Ink*.

I would like to thank John Kinsella for his encouragement during the four years in which this book was written, and also Patrick Buckridge and Mhairead MacLeod for their editorial assistance.

I The Forest

Narrative of a Leaf

Start with suspense.
Picture an average leaf
humming carelessly in the wind.
It doesn't know what's coming.
Complications.
June frost, drought,
delinquent insects.

It is hard work, putting food on the table,
growing a tree.
Forgoing the luxury of individualism.
This is the heroism
of the ordinary leaf.

With no rehearsal, jump into the void,
fall like an angel
with half a parachute.
Whether raked or left in peace
keep busy in community service.
Be an example without being didactic.
A kind of glory.

Literary Forests

for John Kinsella

1. THE LAST OF THE MOHICANS

It was a forest of 'fantastic limbs
painted against a starry zenith'.
Hawkeye grazed the arm of murderous
Le Subtil, the 'red devil', with a running shot.
'I rubbed the bark off a limb'
he said, disappointed.
The sisters clung to one another,
saw arms and legs above and all around—
the woods had eyes and mouths.

Alice was disposed to laugh.
But Cora felt comforted by their guide's
hunting-shirt of forest green and amber—
the hues of the undergrowth.
She had seen hunters of the boudoir
at home—snakes who flickered their
tongues at young women in the season.
But the pathfinder's guile was weathered,
stripped of predatory glances.
His moccasins winked like gem-beetles,
like butterflies drying their wings.
He was earnest, yes, and driven,
in a soon to be modern way,
yet more inviting than
a quadrille and French musk.

Cora waved, though ambiguously:
a square of handkerchief, pennant,
that could have been encouragement
to the hardy colonists
or a warning to the forest, still

crouched beside the treadmill water,
to be more alert in future.
The lace cotton fell and fluttered
like a premonition
for one whose hair was like
the 'tendrils of the vine'.
Always alien to these parts,
but soon embraced by a shroud
of silver birch fine as her skin.

2. The Children of the New Forest

Only as adults did we realise
that this forest was a lie—the natural
did not reside in the divine right of kings.
We were led astray, along with those
children gobstruck by a king's wig,
his heart yearning for his subjects
but distracted by his new blue garters.

The Puritans had a higher regard for trees
than the Cavaliers. Cromwell found the forest
solid, dependable, unadorned by vanity.
'How have you lived so long,' he queried an oak.
The oak stood, plain dressed, rooted in the
commonwealth of humus and worms,
the fallen acorns, and kept its counsel.
It was then Oliver knew he would triumph,
die, and one day triumph again.

3. Robinson Crusoe

Crusoe looked at a tree and saw congealed
within it a sled, five stout barrels, a fort,
something to notch the working days on.
And Friday, he wasn't a wood sprite,
noble savage, or guide to botanical mysteries,
but an absence of application and shaping.

The coconut trees bore fruit in their idle way
unconscious of the beauty of effort,
the soul's joy in double entry book-keeping.
Behind them indistinguishable groves hovered,
hissing with insects, promiscuous scents,
backward-looking, taboo.

So Crusoe, stranded on a thin strip of sand,
a beach reeking with cannibal vulgarity,
shaded his face with one hand, searched an ocean
of featureless blue, both changing and unchanged,
which might one day puff its cheeks and send ships,
wooden angels flying for captains of industry,
the bold ecstatic prayer that is engineering.

4. The Wind in the Willows

Mole saw clearly that he was an animal of tilled field and hedge-row, linked to the ploughed furrow, the frequented pasture, the lane of evening lingerings, the cultivated garden-plot. For others the asperities, the stubborn endurance, or the clash of actual conflict, that went with Nature in the rough . . . Kenneth Graham

It was Rat who explained
the industrial revolution to Toad—
how it had no business except in
the consuming pleasures of agriculture.

But more dangerous than the machine,
where the plough turned for home,
lay the Terror of the Wild Wood.
A place of confusion and whispers,
malevolent yellow eyes.
Here stoats and ferrets
carelessly spoke uneducated English
and mocked their social betters.

Mole had escaped the Wood, of course,
but some summer evenings, sipping tea
from bone china, or sweeping his pantry,
he felt the pull of the wildness
that had led him there
on that fateful night.

Oh to be an animal at ease in the dark
he thought—a bold Woods Mole.
To walk where there are no paths,
to swagger and give back-chat like a fox,
and never cower at the brush of an owl's wing.

Oh to meander beneath the high branches,
instead of where hedge-rows martial
the meadows in lock-step,
and thin lines of willows despair and slump.

In the Wood there were no privatising rabbits
charging tolls to enter back lanes.
Even the slight weasel felt safe there.
He sat on the river bank, among Comfrey
and pink willow-herb, and grew restless,
taller, more supple.

What on Earth, he wondered aloud,
is a mole doing with a checked
kitchen apron round his waist,
or a Harrods hamper of cakes
and ginger beer?
A ripple of musky heat drifted
from the just visible distance
and he drank it in till his chest rose.
He set off across the fields
towards the rocks and brambles,
this time whistling an old tune
that was sure to be the password.
Golden light already welled
in the paleness of his eyes.

The Black Forest

1.

There are postcards in Freiburg
about the acid rain that drifts in from England:
'Baumsterben—na und?'—
a satirical cartoon of a German family
striding happily in Lederhausen
through a brown, stubbled moonscape—
'Wir lassen ums den Schwarzwald nicht miesmachen!'

To the north a farmer ploughs his field
a child follows a hare.
They stumble over rusting metal,
disappear in a shout, a shock of air.

2.

The forest broods over the town—
every fifty metres along the broad track
wooden signs with stick figures demonstrate
callisthenics for hikers under the pines.
Athletic youths in serious boots
and bright backpacks
stop and bend to the left and right,
reach their toes.
Nature with a purpose.

3.

In the more remote valleys
the green is so dense it comes alive.
There are calls of something
half-human, half-beast.
There are drowned women
caught in the folds of their flowing gowns,

who lie in wait
at the bottom of mountain pools
to trap the thirsty traveller.
The pine-needles provide warmth
for the wood-wives.
They recoil from Carroway seeds,
church bells, or the colour red.
If they happen to hear the sound of a machine
they will lose their minds.
Each year they retreat farther
into the heart of the woods, the ground mist.

   4.

Deeper forest—dark and still.
only faint light filters here.

After midnight a demon fell from the sky
trailing fire, and here it has lain for sixty years.
Black water and moss quenched the flames
and gathered it in.
The demon stretches out its arms
but cannot move, its back broken,
its riders sunk into earth.
The forest accepts the new creature.
This metal it can assimilate—
it takes on snow, fire, acid.

The demon with its concentric circles
becomes first an offering,
then a forest god, finished with the sky.
Learns to grow its own leaves
nourished by humus,
  breathes through lichen and toadstools,

shivers a lung spark, a premonition
that moves among the branches
until it reaches the village
with its tiny, speckled lamps,
its lovers who stare at the moon.
The elderly listen for the drone of more demons
come to search for the lost one.

Eventfully the wood-wives smell the demon
and rub their faces with a potion
of sour berries, fungus and rain water
so they can approach it.
With their wrinkled eyes they see the furnace
of a factory in Manchester,
the demon strung with bright ribbons
and cheering men.
They steal away the bones
and bury them in peat moss.

The Conservative Forest

for Bruce Dawe

This is a family-values forest. The red-checked table cloth
is spread on grass where the canopy has been removed.
The sun shines as required, a hygienic space to celebrate
freedom, strong government, luminous freeways.

The elitists wanted this closed to ordinary people,
and left for soap-fearing ferals, anti-social bushwalkers.
But now it is accessible, with tables made of eucalypt,
trees making a contribution, in full employment.

Long gone is the anarchy of wilderness, the over-excited mind.
Discipline is learned from a neat row of firs, a line of swings
under the Big Axe. The kids, Andrew and Emma, draw houses
with chimney smoke on paper the wood-chips have provided.

But do not relax. Be wary of seductive tunes from the foliage,
of horns and pipes, dangerous nymphs with plausible stories.
They whisper of peace won without cost in blood.
They meddle with gender and leave the young confused.

See them in jester's cloaks, their hair like snakes,
lodged in tree tops or introspective undergrowth,
cursing the honest toil of chainsaw and bulldozer,
the strong orange arms, the friendly giants.

At night you may hear gentle keening, the pioneers whose
prayers and sweat cleansed the scrub, made the ground
sweet for cattle and wheat, braved the savages and gypsies,
carved an asylum under stars for those who followed.

Today is a reunion, mum in her apron, children with toy guns,
dad will polish the four wheel drive. The park awaits our return,
invites us to enjoy the fruits of our labours. Sausages and wine,
the glow of the sacred barbecue. A fire to reflect our hunger.

The Imperial Forest

In the jungles of the Amazon and Peru
Cinchona officianlis the fever tree,
and *Hevea brasilienus* the weeping tree,
in fragrant yellow and pink flowers
breathe the miasma of morning,
bright-beaked parrots and ginger monkeys.

Malaria-ridden Europe
ringed by swamps and marshes
sends out its scrapers and slicers,
the blazing-eyed plant-hunters of Kew.
They carry their collecting bags and bottles,
traps and scales, jostle with
Colonial rubber tappers and Jesuit traders
to steal the Indians' secrets.

The Jesuits argue up an antidote,
but protestants prefer to die of fever
than drink the papist potion.
Oliver Cromwell sweats his way
to heaven. But the empire-makers
see a way to make the rainforest safe
from boiling blood, as temperate
and waterproof as a men's club.

Joseph Banks, emperor of pressed plants
strolls through his London garden
for miles and miles,
writes sycophantic letters to the mad king,
sings a song for everything
useful in the vegetable kingdom;
the economic crop in E major.

The Brazilian jungles shrink back, while
the Indian and Malayan plantations grow fat.
The colour of the season is quinine.
Cartwheels newly shod with rubber
speed gold to the bank.

The doctors howl and scowl
and flap their white coats.
Bleeding their patients was a good earner.
They continue to tie off arteries,
collect heart-juice in cups,
denounce a powder too cheap,
too light for mystery.

The mosquitoes and syphilitic merchants
scream too, as they crouch in their
respective lairs. But the merchants recover.
Adventure and profit are multiplied
by the fruits of bark and seed,
the magic, once-secret garden,
a home-brand pharmacopeia.

St Martin and St Boniface Destroy the Forest Gods

To show the heathens how utterly powerless were the gods in whom they placed their confidence, Boniface felled the oak sacred to the thunder-god Thor, at Geismar, near Fritzlar. He had a chapel built out of the wood and dedicated it to the prince of the Apostles. The heathens were astonished that no thunderbolt from the hand of Thor destroyed the offender, and many were converted. The fall of this oak marked the fall of heathenism. [Catholic encyclopaedia]

As the German people watched
with horror in their bowels,
beefy Boniface pushed up the sleeves
on his freckled forearms
and chopped down their sacred oak.
Flushed, he leapt onto the oozing stump
and standing with his feet far apart
declared:
'You see now, heathen spittle,
my God is more powerful than yours.
The axe is more pure than the hammer.
Your childish legends,
your superstitious regard for nature,
these are abominations
which the one God who is three gods
(and that should impress you)
can not bear to witness.'

He took the shattered branches
and patiently built a small chapel.
There the people sat huddled and silent
while Boniface told them again
about the fits of jealousy
that heaved in God's bosom
whenever he looked down
and saw them fondling herbs,
or on their knees before forest giants
more tangible than he.

The lament of the tree spirits,
the groans of the oak martyrs
still filtered through the church's
narrow windows on a still night.
But the heathens, faces closed as nutshells,
were too terrified to listen
to the forest stories anymore.
Anyway, they told themselves, it was
probably just the Holy Spirit poking around,
like an aging, fussy caretaker.

Martin, Bishop of Tours
was less robust than Boniface.
Thin-shanked and mounted on a horse,
he specialised in the killing of pine trees.
Some of the more resilient pagans
tied him to their favourite conifer,
then hacked at another, nearby pine
so it would fall his way
and crush him.

But such irony was lost on God.
At the last moment
he sprang like a great panther
and pushed the toppling tree
back upon the people
so that many were slaughtered.
The pagans had a meeting
and reluctantly agreed that
a sky-riding monster,
though invisible,
must in the end be obeyed.

The humiliation of the forest,
fear of the old wood-spirits
both hoarse and sweet,
drilled slowly into their hardening hearts,
to be passed down evermore.

Sigurd is Instructed by the Birds

Sigurd agreed to roast
the dragon's heart,
though he could not look
the animal in the face.
Through averting his eyes
he burned his fingers,
and slipped them in his mouth
to ease the pain.
He thought he saw the dragon smile.

But the heart's savoury blood
had flecked his hand,
and tasting it
he now understood
the language of birds.

Given the pulpit, the birds
did not know where to stop.
There was so much to warn him of:
the evil of those closest to you,
the whereabouts of treasure,
the silliness of heart-eating.

He knew he could ride
through fire to find Brynhildr,
cut her from her tight armour
and warrior nights,
lick the honey from her thighs.

But instead he made a bower
from oak leaves, and lay under the tree
where the birds gave
their lectures in summer semester.
In good time he became Sigurd,
postgraduate of the woods,
where there are no exams or fools.

Brynhildr Becomes a Nature Goddess

When Sigurd left
the trees were full of his promises
roosting like white egrets.
But I have had enough of my bed—
the sleep-thorn chained me there,
more corpse than Valkyr.

Much to do relearning the seasons,
let alone a million spring flowers.
Then Sigurd returned,
or at least his facsimile.
Singed grey by the wall of flames,
Gunnar talked me to the boudoir.

I found out about this betrayal
when bathing in the river with
Gunnar's unbalanced sister Gudrun.
Her gold-crazed brother,
stomach distended
with wolf and adder flesh,
sliced my Sigurd slim as a boy.

Now you must embrace
the sword and pyre
said the Valkyr handbook:
but I had taken enough sleep.

Light with grief, my body
was borne against the current
with full swan escort.
A fox took me to the gentle woods
and my fertile contemplation.

I walked out of my body,
into the same sunshine which feeds
Gudrun's wine-cups
and my cloud-tossed empire.

Brisbane, 1959–1960

For David Malouf

1.

Each night the bush moves closer
to the suburb and the mosquito net,
and in winter the wolves come.

Outside my parent's house,
the sweet-pea trellis, Oleanders,
dissolve into fir trees.

At dawn the pack is drunk with moon,
running the rim of hills that holds us here.

Still half in sleep, lungs swollen,
I cough phlegm into a china bowl.
The grey tree tops are jagged, as obvious
to me as paw prints on linoleum.

2.

A year later, trying to cook sausages
in the bush a mile away,
I bring fire to the dry slopes.

It plunges over Weller's Hill,
fingers the porous wire fence
that surrounds my primary school.

I slide down a road-cutting to escape,
cycle home recklessly, wait for police,
firemen, to knock at our door.

3.

Fire, asthma, the genial doctor's night visits
to administer adrenalin injections.

Lizards appear again on charred bark,
beetles luminous as watch dials.
But no wolves rise from the ashes.

Clouds

In the past, there was a landowner who used the shadows of clouds on the hillside as a way of deciding the shape for planting his woods!
SCOTTISH FORESTRY BOOKLET

Here the contours are hunched hills
of rock and grass, as if, running to
mark out the edges of the cloud
with red ribbons on stakes, the
landowner trips and falls,
lies cursing the wind that
swallows his blueprint
for birch and pine,
hazel and rowan,
before planting
can inscribe
his great
idea.

There are problems that reside
in taking Nature as our guide.
We can not trace the totality
of the sun's imperial survey,
the golden eagle's wing
sky-carving through
mountain top mists,
butterfly swarms,
or on its plinth
the circling
sundial fin
shading
all our
days.

Crusoe Revisited

[the civilised world] could not, with all its enjoyments, restore him to the tranquillity of his solitude.
                     RICHARD STEELE — *reporting Selkirk's words*

Alexander Selkirk stood trembling
on the sand, excrement dribbling
down his legs, his hair matted
with the fish leavings of seagulls.
Once rescued, he gestured
to the sailors to draw closer,
but could only moan and mumble
half-words. That half not misplaced
in the forest, the nights with no sound
except jaw crunch and rustle,
his sleeping bag of cats and rats.

～

I danced with the cats in the moonlight,
he tried to tell his rescuers.
A jig from a wedding in Largo.
And the cats, less fleet than he,
threw themselves about as best they could.
Always the smoke of pimento wood curled
up from the cliff, ambiguous in its aim.
His bible and books swam away from him,
signs with less purchase than shellfish,
or his budding Spanish turnips.

Returned to Scotland, a pirate hero,
he first eloped with shy Sophia,
then lived by himself in a cave again.
But this cave whispered of madness,
not the 'tranquillity of solitude'.

Once he had carved his name on palm trees
to distinguish them from him.
But now the trees were aloof and coy.

He beckoned the sailors closer
and they marvelled at his long hair,
his cap of white fur, the tropical odour.
But they heard only the vocabulary
of loneliness as he tried to confess his
copulation with goats.

For a serviceable pair of trousers
he would gladly have traded
his Enlightenment epiphany:
namely, that the 'primitive' is neither
degradation nor celebration.
Just silhouette. The tree-line at sunset,
bats charred black on the moon,
the ice edge of a storm cloud.
The village Kirk would not accept
this as wisdom — but Heaven's
hard men had never dressed
in rotting sail cloth.

His knife wore down to its back.
He made a new knife from the
iron hoop of a wine barrel,
washed up in the morning
like a slow letter from home.
In delight he thanked the waves,
and they, curled upon his praise,
brought driftwood, their alphabet
in froth fragments, and his new voice.

Death will be Unsighted

I come to the forest again
this anchor to earth
this complicated light,
and beneath its prodigious green
stand still in the hope
death will be unsighted
and slink back to the creaky staircase,
the level crossing, or beery pub.

Wild plums grow in tangled weight
each September, and over there
is a courtesy of wildflowers
where the thinking animal falters
beneath a flock of parrots,
is suddenly wrapped
in the same instinctive colours,
the details of existence brilliant,
more precise,
walking on dusk.

Statues

Settled on an island paradise
the Polynesians chopped
each day in the forests
to make mountains of firewood,
elegant canoes, religious statues,
until the last trees were gone
and the earth blew away.

The Vikings who gutted Iceland,
the pioneers who salted our outback
could not imagine the future either.

Some of the trees have become
books on ancient ritual, magic wisdom.

There is chanting in the valley
as I drive back from New South Wales
along the Mt Lindsay highway.
Kites and orange dragons
circle a bonfire built
in the arms and legs
of a giant scarecrow.

I'd like to say to them:
we need science and statistics now
for protection,
not statues.

The same night my headlights
find peripheral ghosts of Mountain Ash
while a billion specks of soil
settle on the sea
like a blush.

Northern Hairy-Nosed Wombat

The suburbs breed assassins
in claustrophobic backyards.

And beyond this smudge
of remnant woodland
is the circling tractor,
the stamp of hoofed feet.

The suits calculate the rural vote.
Iron necklaces level the west,
no burrow deep enough.

Gangway

At the abattoir pigs and cattle
move forward in the queue until
they stand second from the front.
Hormones flood
the arteries and brain,
the electricity of a false sky
as they turn to the sun.

At the shopping centre
old people whisper the latest
death of an acquaintance,
smooth the red check tablecloth
with both hands, feel a pressure
inside the rib cage:
the words *was* and *me*.

In the Tasmanian forest
a bloodwood loses skull and feet,
clavicle and vertebrae,
woodchips for those who
are allowed obituaries.

The concrete is slippery
near the steel gangway.
As when I wake at 4.00 a.m.
and see a begging light
sleep-walk towards
the grey swamp cypress
in our back yard.

In Praise of Bears

To national parks at frontier's end
free campers from the heartland wend

seated in their Humvee motor,
here comes lunch from Minnesota.

To camp sites amble bear and cougar
seeking snacks of fat and sugar

embrace these burghers plump and pink
and tenderly incisors sink.

Such the ethic of these creatures—
they watch no sport nor loll on beaches

but lap the sweet cool stream's libation,
burp titbits of a warrior nation.

We're excremental, not divine,
and in the food-chain reassigned.

All praise the tent's surprise collapse
all praise suave bears who wear red caps

all hail the eyes beyond the fire
reminders of the planet's hire.

Where Texas deer lie trussed on hoods,
vengeance is mine, declare the woods.

Jim Corbett Has the Idea for a National Park

The man-eater took its forty-seventh victim
just west of Chaknakl on the Ramganga River.
It had lain for hours in the undergrowth watching
three young women work the fields with sickles,
tying grass into bundles.
At noon the jungle bounded towards
the one dressed in blue.
She saw striped saplings,
red orchids, blend together.
Her friends screamed to alert the village
but it took her in its jaws
deep into dense tree and scrub jungle
where at first she heard the insects singing.
It partly ate, then left the body,
to sleep off its meal in a bamboo thicket
a hundred yards away.

I purchased a small male buffalo
and staked it beneath a tree
near the tiger's kill. From late afternoon
I sat in the machan with my torch and rifle
fighting off drowsiness
the tendency to make monsters
out of moonlight,
the temptation to sneeze or cough.
Listened for the warning call of the langur,
the jungle's news teller
khok, khok, khoc, knokorror.

My throat was sore from the cold rain
that had drenched me just after dark.
Mosquitoes covered my head
but I resisted the urge to swat them.
I kept my eyes on the forlorn remains,

the scraps of her clothes.
Sometime before dawn
caught in the return of old fever,
I slept like a roosting bird
while the tiger gnawed
through two thick ropes
and dragged the buffalo away.

After breakfast and a bath I put on
the thinnest of rubber soled shoes
and went into the green heat again.
The carpet of leaves was wet and pliable
and I followed the faint blood trail
across a ridge and down into waist-high
bracken beside a creek.
The creature's pug marks were in the mud.
For two hours, creeping along
a ravine choked with thorns and moths,
a shadow among shadows
I stared through trees that could eat me,
brushwood that might rasp
the skin off with its tongue,
felt the clawing
of my scalp from my skull.

I found it, stretched out
under a rock ledge, eyes closed.
I raised the D.B. 400/450
and as I watched the sticky
light between us wavering,
a neat bloodless hole in its head
blurred and closed again,
the orange belly rose and fell
and for an instant I was borne high

as the sun-streaked canopy.
I saw from above a mantle of mist,
the four winds of heaven,
monkey, pheasant and python
gathered at sunset in open glades,
and felt the clinging hillside send
a note of rebuke soft as fur,
the pungent scent of white flowers,
and I could not shoot.

Koreelah Ranges, Northern NSW

Platypus Flat.
A thousand acres bordered by
the Clarence River and Tooloom Creek.
The pine cabin darkens and shrinks,
its oils drained by sun and wind,
that sharp debating team.
Two hundred metres from here
sandy river and rocky stream meet,
rewriting banks in the vernacular,
surgically exposing tree roots.

Blue haze of angophora.
In the granite hills red-tailed cockatoos
split Casuarina nuts in faint punctuation.
This is not soft country;
the walker can be bloodied by lantana
burned by stinging nettles.
Storms bully between the hills,
lift driftwood into branches.

Rural Gothic.
There were gold-mining camps
beside the Tooloom in 1859.
Abandoned shafts remain, half-hidden in bracken,
ringed with stones carried up from the creek.
Three grey tent poles still lean against each other
in skeletal dance.

An intellectually handicapped boy
spent years chained to the farm house
in the next valley, hidden from visitors,
in case the government took him away.
They say a woman was cut down with an axe
before she reached the gate.

Here rifles are carried.
Our neighbour bulldozes his rainforest gully
sugared with bell birds
to thwart the politicians and do-gooders.
Our wire fence is snipped again
so a farmer has free agistment.

He laughs in the Urbenville pub
about Subaru hippies, *academics*.
At night his cattle huddle beneath our cabin,
lean against the stumps dreaming of old age.
We plant parsley and barbed wire.

Semi-lyrical dawn conclusion.
Pygmy bats fly back inside the hut,
Currawongs clatter on the tin roof.
Mist dissolves on polished grass and icy river.
Smoke from the pot-bellied stove
slides through the counterfeit sun.
The canoe drifts on a slow current
under bottle-brush and whip-bird air.
Platypus make their jack-knife exit
and the water is flecked with crimson stamens,
stutter of water-spider.

With a mattock we dig our morning toilet
on the slope beside musky lantana.
The bush is already as talkative as an exile.
In the open there is a roof of birds.
We squat and watch the river,
how the orange flowers, our sweat,
the wood smoke, map the hour.

Ecological Love Poem

This poem arrives at the function unsure if it is
under-dressed. It glances around the room hoping
to see someone it knows. Relieved, it recognises
the romantic image of the tree, the archetype of fruit.
The lyric, woman and tree are old friends.

You and I prefer a sceptical heart. Alarmed by the fuzzy
retreat into the personal that swells poets' tongues.
Others deploy terror-management theory, incense
or neediness. But in the space between tough hope
and another year, I write the endless charm of your face.

Here is rational love, tree song, this tunnel of light
through the late bush, as we fall to silence.
The parrot flash and purple sky are almost invisible,
and we know about trust—look, that glistening creek
ahead is really a weakened trunk infested with beetles.

I can no longer disappoint her, now she and the poem
are the same. No pygmy Wordsworths scurry through
this undergrowth, scribbling in lavender notebooks;
no tiny Tennyson conjures maidens in sultry paperbark.
We make our own ecology in a youthful century.

The poem and the forest have emotional intelligence.
Shoeless she walks through them, words crackle underfoot.
'Being in the world' will bring us home, my love,
after we have made pilgrimage to each other,
to the eucalypts which burn, and hoist their colours.

May Gibbs in the New Suburbs

At the edge of the cities are the new estates:
Forest Place, Forest Dale, Forest Hill,
Forest Ridge, Forest Grove, Forest Ville.
On Saturdays at 9.00 a.m. the men go outside
and perform the lawnmower tango
like a quirky Australian movie.

In each estate there is a small park
and a set of monkey bars,
as if children allowed to climb an actual tree
might suddenly decompress
like a punctured plane passenger,
morph into rogue gumnuts,
or bee-struck blossom.

Plantation—Glasshouse Mountains

In the pine plantation
are fresh trail-bike tracks,
an empty shotgun cartridge

windowless car bodies.
Mt Coonowrin's dislocated neck
hung over her like a bruise.

They bound her hands,
told her to smile,
icy air fell down around her.

She must have looked up
just here, seen something
move through the branches

though there were no parrots,
or someone calling from the
kitchen, just a savage door

her body passed through,
a movie of spiders on the skin,
acidic leaf litter.

She sits on the deck
beside the borer-riddled pines,
and a mountain going nowhere.

Anatomy of a Forest

This is 'dry sclerophyll'.
Unlike rainforest, every plant here
earns its place. Australian,
it feeds on self-doubt, north-facing.

Ironbark on a stony ridge,
Eucalyptus crebra,
its thin leaves pendulous, back-lit.

Pragmatism seeps up
through the red trunk core,
its real estate is soil, water,
not superstition or justice.
Its conversation as disciplined
as the Stoics.

Below the ridge, heraldry:
ferns, twiners, ground orchid,
lichen, fungi, wombat berry,
like smudged paint in the grass.

In the gullies wasp and snail,
larvae, tick, sawfly, rodent.
Eat and be eaten.
The moral code of wartime.

This may seem a dysfunctional culture.
But no counselling is required
in the leaf-litter, no social safety-net.
Experimental theatre thrives though.
Millipede amnesia,
scorpion reflex,
dragonfly flamboyance.

*Those who see all creatures
in themselves.*
Can it be possible.
To trade anatomy, skin,
nascent wings,
the messages of scent.
To undress our mind along the high ridge
of ironbark trees,
join the wider debate of August?

Public Liability

In the city fathers' nightmares
branches tangle above a narrow path
and they are the lost child again,
running through a forest
from animal noises,
hearts frozen by moonlight
and the hanging tree.

The Council severs twenty-one branches
from the jacaranda on our footpath.
Hundreds of pollards, armless zombies,
stand in grotesquery.

At Newfarm Park
a particularly vicious Moreton Bay Fig
is contained by a low fence
more securely than Kong.
Mothers hurry their children past
the giant, fecund beast.

Those left standing arrange their limbs
to project benevolence, avuncular interest.
Try not to stir alarmingly in the breeze.

In the nightmares of officialdom,
buds start to bubble through white paint,
erupt under faux Tuscan paving.
Tree scouts are sent ahead
to direct the advance guard,
to extract Intelligence
from boulevard collaborators.
The Tallowwood and Scribbly Gum
shake with ecstasy,
feel the weight of their purpose.
Rank upon rank they descend from the hills.
Close in upon the city coffee shops
where architects are lost in space.

Recording the Birds

for Helen Horton

It took twenty years to record them all.
Near Alice Springs the Chiming Wedgebill,
at Cooktown the Curlew Sandpiper
just back from Siberia.
She trudged through Melaleuca swamps
with a microphone muffled in foam,
interpreting hollows in dead gums,
scanning the river bank for Rainbow Bee-eaters.

Recognising secondary calls
on the tape wasn't difficult.
Often it was the Double-barred finch,
or flocks of wood swallows passing through.
The droning jet and dog bark
could not be expunged.

Rising two hours before dawn
on the Lamington Plateau
she walked eleven kilometres
towards the mountain top.
Behind the rain and fog
Antarctic Beeches were withdrawn
as amnesia, the bush taciturn.
But among dense ferns and tussocks
she captured a clear five minutes
of the Rufous Scrub-bird's piercing notes.
Took the tape home in triumph,
played it back, but it had gone,
though she'd made no technical error.

Just an unnamed murmur,
and the faint breathing in and out
of the forest's lungs.
Something inarguably huge.
Approaching nearer
and drawing back again.

Salt

Amongst these old gums
are cliffs so sheer
they draw an ocean in.

You hear it by late afternoon—
the pulse of waves in the tree tops,
and a taste of salt on the breath.

Two hundred miles from the coast,
yet water presses the horizon
where yesterday there was desert.

Hard to keep your balance
in the brief hollow between
blue-green pillars

of wash carrying seeds,
the flotsam of Egypt, Belsen,
a world chemistry.

The waves calm by morning
leaving two faint moons,
and now we are floating under

a scarlet tide, laconic sky,
inventing stories of an
afterlife, a miraculous comeback.

As we stand under old-growth trees
something shines brighter in the aviary
of human. We are taken down

by the undertow, able to breathe in
the first tropical sea. We school together,
called into awareness, brilliant.

We ride the flood, no longer anxious
to outstay our genes, sheltered from
the weather of personal survival.

The Art of Memory

Once you tell yourself
that enough old growth
forest is left

that warnings
of endangered species
are emotive

that replanting
can resuscitate
a complex ecology

that science can cure
a sweating planet,
you're on a roll.

The back yard looks
out of focus,
the wife and kids more distant

until you are sitting
on the hypothesis of a chair
in a room stripped bare.

You click the
remote control but
the family is hiding
or extinct.

At Christmas the loggers
bring you a hamper:

'Can't see anything, mate'
you tell them without panic

in your voice.
They slap you
where your back
might have been

then they walk back up the drive.
Maybe they're waving.

The Lost Valley

for Daniel Defoe, John Clare and Adrian Mitchell

A private jet passes
above remote rainforest.
Stirred by global warming,
a storm clutches it into cloud.
In an eye blink, a flock of birds
has filled the twin turbines.

The handsome pilot dies
but five survive the crash:
Alexandra the prize-winning engineer,
Jill the Reality TV producer,
Gerhard the disciplined explorer,
John the slightly autistic scientist,
Damien the bad poet.

Alexandra designs a multi-level
loft-complex from saplings,
thatched grass, rubber tree sap
and the plane's plastic windows.

Jill irritates them by saying
over and over: 'Oh my *God*!
This is just like *Survivor*'.
No one will make an alliance with her.

Gerhard explores the valley
from 8.30 a.m. to 4.30 p.m. every day
but finds there is no way out.
They are surrounded by sheer cliffs
of slippery granite.

John doesn't speak at all
and seems alienated

by the determined positivity of the group.
He sleeps apart in a hollow tree.

Damien writes a poem choked
with similes and rhetorical questions:
'Again the sunset was ripe as a tomato—
so why does my tortured mind explode
and explode with regret and yearning?'

He has explosive yearning for Alexandra.
Both being 'artists' and 'thinkers',
they find themselves drawn together.

The packets of peanuts salvaged
from the aircraft run out.
They visit John and delegate him
to find bush tucker. Almost invisible
in the undergrowth and mossy trees
he notes which berries the animals eat,
digs for sweet roots and yams,
learns the secrets of this kitchen.
Because the others are preoccupied
with their meetings and starred agendas,
he also becomes the cook.

That winter, a ghostly fever seeps in from
the jungle. They lie moaning in their hammocks.
John crawls out into the forest
and returns with a nettle he boils
for two days. It cures them all.

Jill finds her digital camera in the wreck
and makes a reality program about
the other four. She follows them everywhere,
hoping to capture an intimate moment.

She soon captures Alexandra and Damien
going at it like hogs on heat.
They splutter and protest,
then replay themselves
repeatedly on the tiny screen.
Gerhard goes and sits in the cold creek.

With nothing left to yearn for,
Damien runs out of inspiration and catches
writer's block. He also catches impotence.
John finds him a purple berry
that restores his stamina, but by then
Alex is 'collaborating'with Gerhard
who has gone into property development.
After all, he has surveyed the whole valley
and knows the prestige locations.

He and Alex build two more high-rise units
a kilometre away, in case other planes crash
and a niche market opens up.
Anticipation is the secret of business.

A year later things are deteriorating.
The camera's battery has died
and Jill has a depressive illness
none of John's berries can cure.
Alex and Gerhard build a canal development
by diverting a waterfall. They call it New Eden.
Damien stops brooding and writes
the publicity brochures. 'You can start again
in a new paradise,' they promise;
'Your minds will explode with happiness'.

But no other plane crashes
and the jungle starts inching over
their shopping mall
like a Cambodian temple.

Just in time, Gerhard discovers an escape route.
Behind the waterfall there is a secret tunnel
spiralling upwards. With a system of pulleys
and strangler vine ropes he is confident
he can reach the top and bring rescue.

John withdraws even more into his silence.
He will not help with the frantic vine plaiting.

He goes deeper through the jungle
and listens to its complex gossip.
From a scarlet trumpet flower
he concocts a potion that slows
all commerce from the heart's tributaries.

Mixes it with their sorbet that night.

It is designed so they feel no pain
but drift into cleansing dreams.
Their stiff morning faces, as he gazes at them,
carry blissful smiles.

John puts some potion in his pocket
and takes one last walk to the creek.

For a long while he rests by the water
that flows over paintbox stones.
A late afternoon shower wakes him.
The small leaves glisten like glass.

He puts aside the poison.
A question lays its bait instead.
He wonders why the living
must always eat with the dead.

The Fairy-Tale Forest

The Wolf did a course in anger
management and entered mediation
with the victims of his crime.
It turned out he had been abandoned
as a cub and saw Riding Hood's
grandma as a neglectful mother-figure.

Hansel and Gretel slowly recovered
in hospital from sugar diabetes,
wore fire-resistant overalls.
With industrial blowtorches they
melted all the chocolate houses
dotted on the magic forest maps.

Snow White set up a rehabilitation program
for witches who really *wanted* to change.

Even Pooh and Piglet studied Hospitality
at a polytechnic, conducted daily tours
by golf cart of the Hundred Acre Wood
('Get your souvenir pots of hunny at the exit')
denied they had ever believed in Heffalumps
or trembled at a noise in the night.

All the woods were accessible and safe
as Woolworth's. At night they were patrolled
by axemen, monitored by CCTV. But sometimes
the forest folk peered out at the trees hung
with safety lanterns, paths lined with hand rails,
and yearned for unimaginable menace.

The Man Who Couldn't See Colours

On Saturday morning, the facilitator says there are only two emotions: Fear and Love.

We learn to meditate, to visualise a scene from nature: a mountain creek, or pristine beach. We are told to visualise the colours of the spectrum, one by one, from Red through to Violet. A man puts his hand up. He can't see colours. The facilitator says to him: just release your Fear.

Single people check out other single people. We are told a lot of new relationships begin on these weekends. At morning tea, the man who can't see colours stands alone.

That afternoon, we each have to get up in front of the group and say what we most want in our lives. A middle-aged computer salesman with a gold bangle says he wants Love, and stares at a pretty schoolteacher in the front row. The man who can't see colours says he wants to lose his Fear. We all clap and he sits down and wipes his face with a handkerchief. In the break for orange juice and high fibre biscuits, gold bangle asks the teacher for her phone number. She experiences annoyance, which is neither fear nor love.

On Sunday we form two lines and then everyone in turn passes blindfolded between the lines, being hugged or patted by the human gauntlet we pass. Gold bangle goes through twice.

We all lie on our backs with our eyes closed and soft music plays. The facilitator tells us to think about the parent who never gave us enough Love. He says, think of the parent who neglected us. He says let out the anger, because that is one of the clever disguises used by Fear. People start to weep. The music gets louder and louder. Gold bangle beats the carpet hard with his fists and shouts: 'You bastard, dad! You bastard!'

I open one eye: everyone but me is writhing on the carpet and sobbing. The music softens. The facilitator tells us our parent is reaching out to us now. We can reach out and hug them back, even the dead ones. People are now sniffling and making little noises of joy. Except the man who can't see colours—he makes no sound at all.

We all line up again for a farewell hug. There is a buoyant mood in the room. My ex-partner, who did the course last year, has been invited back for the final session of this year's course. She has brought her ex-husband, Colin, who still hates me. She hugs my new partner. She hugs me. Colin hugs my new partner. Colin hugs me. His big soft stomach presses into me. I feel a migraine starting.

I go into the meditation room and sit on the multi-coloured cushions. I visualise a north Queensland rainforest. There is a small shining stream. Overhanging bottlebrushes thick with red flowers dip their thin leaves into the water. Striped finches sing inside the safety of the thicket.

Then Colin appears on the other side of the stream. He is angry and has a shotgun and is blasting finches out of the trees. If I'm not careful he will see me hiding behind this meditation log.

I open my eyes, I am still the only one in the room with the cushions. I steady my breathing, close my eyes again and re-focus.

Now the man who can't see colours appears on the bank of the shining creek. He is stumbling along on his own. As he passes, blossoms fall and dissolve. The green drains from every leaf in sight. He walks on, emotionless, impenetrable, beneath invisible trees.

The Need for Seclusion

... to be designated wilderness is for it to be at least a day's walk across ...
                                      —Robert Rankin

The soul is uplifted, the powers of intelligence seem to widen ...
                                      —Horace Benedict De Saussure

When the forest behind
is as deep as the forest ahead,
light intensifies,
foliage relaxes,
the day lengthens
on a single pebble,
wilderness enters the skin.

Once more monsters roar
at night in the marshland,
five day gales
throw exhausted birds into the sea
like a distress signal.
Again we lie huddled
to the curvature
of the earth.

Though we lack the migratory path
of geese to the wetlands,
our radar leads us back
to the first database,
evergreen and deciduous,
a mental woodland
many days wider than
Thoreau's cabin on the pond.

This is the university of leaves,
and we are untenured,
so necessarily charming.
We start to network, laugh at jokes
to show our learning,
clever, but careful
not to be over-familiar.

Fontainbleau Forest

Six months after a too hasty marriage.
That afternoon in Fontainbleau Forest
wet leaves clung to our backs
like evasive answers.

The descent into habit was subtle
as the drifting of spores in sunlight.

A forest without beasts
or birdsong is a dead place.
The marks in the mud were of
prancing horses, carts, pistols
and religion, soldiers' boots.
Not a real forest after all.

We tried to get lost, but kept finding
the track to the railway station.
The trees were a carnival tent,
we the acrobats of romance.

A year later, from the highest point
on the ruins of Kenilworth Castle,
we saw a red blossom on the horizon,
the baying of hounds
the blood-trail coming closer
and we were caught,
half-way across the river,
breathless, looking back.

Bedtime Story

Once upon a time in a sunny honey land,
the government took a big white car
and drove out to a farmer's property.
The minister and his two young advisers
wearing new black suits got out.

'You must stop clearing remnant vegetation', they said.
'Why should I?' said the farmer.
'Because the soil out here is paper thin.
Because you are causing salinity
and erosion that degrade the land
for you and all the generations who follow'.
The farmer crossed his arms.
'But we have always done it this way'.
'That's the problem' said the government, 'if you keep clearing,
there will be no more farming possible on this marginal land'.

The farmer took his hat off and put it back on.
'Then you must compensate me'.
'Let's get this straight' said the government,
'You want taxpayers to give money to you
so you will stop destroying the land?'
'That's right,' said the farmer, 'you're not slow'.
'But why should they?' said the government.
'It's called the primacy of the individual', said the farmer
with conviction, 'I read it in a political pamphlet'.
'Well, okay', said the government, looking glum,
'Maybe *then* you will vote for us'.

They all sat together and watched the orange sun.
It was starting to set over livid stubble.
The car drove away quickly in a small dust cloud.
'Vote for you?' said the farmer to the horizon.
And his laugh chased the cloud for a while.

Tree-planting

In old pasture above the
widening grin of erosion
we planted a thousand seedlings.

There was both laughter
and reverence in the work.
Children knelt, excited and earnest.

We looked up at rolling cumulus
and saw the tree shepherds
march down from Fanghorn
to inspect the day's work,
their gnarled trunks heavy
with medals from the old regime.
The grass bent, then straightened
where they passed.

We weekend planters
will not live to see these twigs
grow to an army.
But each time we drive by
we will feel the consolation
of our brief journey
to the underground,
our return as temporary gods,
the only way we can.

Under the Cover of Shared Pleasures

Under the cover of shared pleasures
we indulge our forest passions.
We walk the bush collegially with others,
remark the mistletoe in a flooded gum,
while around us true love winks its eye.

The walk is sorority, fraternity, blind man's bluff.
We need group belonging but also the solitary affair,
the sexual thicket where stamen tremble just for us,
pressed leaves hidden in our bottom drawer.

We go home, hail our partners,
keep the libidinous forest to ourselves
until the next assignation. For alone
in scented profusion we will yield again,
secretive but pure, lit by magpie song.

Wilderness

A megasaur fed by millions of years.
Granite and fern-tree torso, ears spread
like *monsteria* leaves, eyes red as stars.
Spore and angiosperm swarm in its coat.

Without need for definition it multiplies,
changes colour, wanders all the continents,
trumpets through Devonian, Carboniferous,
Cretaceous—summer seed, winter slush.

At the last second a conscious species crawls out
of the sea. Megasaur scrambles to higher ground,
to the last, febrile gully. Turns to face them there.
The chalk around its falling hangs in the air.

Carbon Dioxide

Refused a passage with Captain Cook,
Preacher Priestley stayed at home.
Instead of bumping along
from coast to coast,
smudging ink, finding things
that had never been lost,
the preacher stared into a jar.
Stared and stared until
clearer than the fires of Hell,
he saw the ghost of 'injured air'.

∽

Each orbit of the sun
sixty billion tons of carbon
is inhaled by the forest.
It breathes out bird wing,
star shadow, oxygen orchids.

Red desert hides the amphibian
until summer rains.
Chanting frogs shoulder upwards
to gulp the sky.

∽

Priestley would have understood.
Our planet lies between
miracle and last soliloquy.
Warm currents circle at night
in a weedy ocean
bright with phosphorous.

We sit in the garage
with our engines running.

Bush Lullaby 2

One waddling wombat, clawed by feral cat
Two lithe lizards, woven in a plait

Three cackling kookaburras, feather potpourri
Four cute koalas, crushed collaterally

Five quivering quolls, withered in the wheat
Six lush lorikeets, remaindered into meat

Seven perky possums, fertilise the furrows
Eight playful platypus, rot within their burrows

Nine crippled kangaroos, mutant crow and currawong
Twenty million swaggies, drowning in a billabong.

II Metamorphosis

The Anteater

The night sky is bright
with rocket fire.
A US spokesperson explains
how our smart technology
is pinpointing the enemy,
as an anteater's tongue
unerringly streaks to the termite,
and plucks it clean from the nest.

But somehow the machines'
IQ is faltering.
Americans are firing at their allies
(though in a friendly way) and each other
and at leaking bundles of termites who
aren't soldiers.

In the desert dawn
a machine with polished snout
sniffs the confusing air.
If it had a heart
it would flirt with indecision.
History beckons us backwards:
we leave the jungle
for the grassy plains,
manipulate sticks,
discover language,
still shriek and shake our paws.
Swift's man-monkeys
rattling our digital spanners.

Walking with Shoulder Bags

That morning, as she walked unseen
through the city, she collected objects
and put them in canvas bags.
Wasteful things on one shoulder,
useful on the other.

She selected a random shout of greeting,
then found disappointment
like large stones on verandas.
Betrayal during the barbeque,
argument in the new kitchen,
habit stalled at the cross roads.

By afternoon she reached farm land,
gathered dark globs of despair
and suspicion, a slice of warm bread.

By now one shoulder was bruised and chaffed.
Its bag bulged with darkness and noise.

A Cattle Egret walked with her for a while,
but she understood little of its conversation.

As the sun fell away
she came to a small stand of acacias,
hung the heavy bag on a low branch
and rested.

The moon came by.
She looked at it
and remembered being here once before;
recognised the song of cicadas,
the hopeful stillness of owls.

The two bags trembled and took off low
like clumsy fruit bats.

She wondered why she hadn't
come back sooner.
And now, there was little time for sleep
if she were to take it all in.
That cryptic tree alone was so subtle
it might take years.

The city that didn't need to sleep
put up its own duller moon
on the skin of a brown river.

Suburban Dinner (1)

You must be congratulating yourself
on that shallow strategy,
the way your hand brushed her arm
as you reached for the vegetables.
Oh yes, I saw it. And before that,
bending down to retrieve a serviette
deliberately dropped by her side.
I know this from your crow-like cunning
at the office; always the loudest call
but first to hop out of the way.
So—it has begun.
Perhaps in a hotel, not too expensive,
with prints of The Hunt on the wall,
and a witty bowl of roses.
Her donkey-headed husband
prattles on and sees nothing.
Though he glances once or twice
at her expensive beauty, neither you
nor he detects the drama here.
I see her lips harden
on the words 'silly mistake'
as she describes
a plagiarism case made a fuss of
in her daughter's class.
She asks me, what should be the penalty
before the ringing of the bell,
the coffee and chocolates.
How does one put a stop to it.

The Investigation (2)

Evidence was displayed for all
to gawk at, like a village stoning:
a restaurant receipt, a careless laugh,
too many showers.
Her friends talked about their renovations
and spilled words like sugar,
all the time thinking:
so I was right not to want more.
The donkey, going for long runs before work
dealt with it in his own way,
and she enrolled in a night class
so he could spend more time with the children.
She only felt angry once,
when the prosecutors said
these were common clues, and hasty,
because she had thought so long
about it, while you had thought so little.
Her husband's own confession
was considered terribly noble—
about the office fling. But it didn't balance,
his heart having gone missing in action.
Now she's left with a feeling
like being dragged over sharp rocks,
and a kind of nausea
when she sees displays of roses.

Taking Off from Cyprus

It is a grainy, low contrast enlargement
made from a small Box Brownie print.
The aeroplane is poised at the start of its run.
A batman with baggy pants stands below the wingtip,
and I can just see the specks of heads
who are the pilot and navigator.

My father is strapped in inches from the windscreen.
He concentrates on balancing the twin throttles
of the Hercules engines.
Too many of his squadron, also experienced pilots,
have died on take-off or landing.
The slewing aircraft wrenched them,
as they fought for slow seconds, from the level air.

Just last week a pilot went to the CO,
requesting a transfer to bombers in Europe
where the survival rates are the lowest.
He explained he did not have the skill to control
the difficult Beaufighter, to protect his aircrew.
The CO, a bank manager from Melbourne,
had him classified ' Lack of Moral Fibre'.

I see there are small clouds on that morning in Cyprus.
My father releases the brakes, roars across the dust
to patrol the glistening Mediterranean,
only a few metres between him and sea.
A kind of anger has built in his belly,
the black dials say something is pure here
but withered on the ground.

It is still there behind the jokes in the Mess,
twenty year old men shouting in their sleep,
a pale gecko on the wall, clicking its tally of time.
All the enemies, known and unknown,
who can attack out of the sun.

Tavistock Square July 7, 2005

We went into the shop to buy a red cap
that said 'Scotland'—a trivial whim stirred
by my first visit to the Highlands, the hills
and still lakes of my grandmother's country.

We had been on our way to the British Library.
As we stood at the counter there was a loud thud.
Must be another gas explosion, I said
to the shopkeeper and we went back outside.

Sirens, police motorcycles, people fumbling
with their cell phones, smoke haze
up the street, a red bus with a crumpled wing
where we would have been walking.

You can't return to your flat tonight
a policeman later explained apologetically.
I asked if I could get my asthma medicine.
He shook his head. 'It's a bit messy there'.

For nine days, rows of forensic police
crawled on hands and knees through the Square
outside our kitchen, searched the Plane trees
and Elms for fragments of bomb and flesh.

There is no moral to luck, but a rationale to whims,
a desire to wear an emblem that connects us with
the past or confirms membership of the present.
The small enthusiasms that make some connection:
watching the news, planning a trip to Kew Gardens,
where I will leave my lucky cap behind on the train.

First Creative Writing Class

Intensely they listen,
and hidden in that group of twenty
will be two or three
in the disguise of madness.
This manifests as a delusion
of artistic destiny, of special powers.
Soon they will announce themselves,
protesting at a slight criticism, or arguing
a revelation denied to the rest.
It does not help them or us,
it splits the sky and defies the sun.
Forceful and heartfelt,
but always less useful
than a metaphor that works.
Be air-traffic controllers first,
or bee-keepers, I want to exhort them.
Try to build a dry stone wall
in cold weather.
The demons you invoke always fumble,
whereas a writer must proceed
with the utmost care,
in both senses of the word.
Clouds drift by the window,
they read their lines to peer applause.
I have only just begun to know
what a cloud is and could be.
Poetry comes without an alibi,
in lightning flashes of sanity.

Do We Have to Read the Set Books?

For Tom Wayman

No. Sorry, we set those books by mistake:
not one has anything to teach you, in fact,
reading other people's work could well
taint or dilute your unique voice.
When you accept the Nobel Prize for literature
people will be awe-struck when you say,
after thanking your still-young mother,
'I did it all without reading books'.

No. Reading books requires you
to concentrate for long periods on your own.
No one should be expected to endure
torture by a small, inanimate object.

No. But you can buy and arrange them
in a neat pile beside your pillow.
During the night knowledge might
leak into your brain like fairy breath.

No. But you can watch the movie of the novel,
which has the plot but leaves out
the boring stuff, and gives you pictures,
so you can rest your imagination.

Yes. Because maybe I should tell you
that books arise from books, and always have,
that books let you into secrets,
take you to places both dark and luminous,
give you the power to read people's minds,
to open, or close, your world.

Six Curses

for Vicki Raymond

These six curses I send.

The first, that you will find fame,
and seduced by flattery and leeches,
take yourself even more seriously.

The second, that you will find love,
throw yourself upon the glossy moment,
and from its shell see narcissism unfurl.

The third, that you will find wealth,
and leave your partner for a younger version
who understands you all too quickly.

The fourth, that you will find hatred,
and having wiped all armies from the plains,
place the cold, hard stone in your pocket.

The fifth, that you will find history,
which is the door to each day, but even
with hindsight be incapable of regret.

The sixth, that you will find certainty,
and gagging on this poisoned feast
suffer the greatest curse of all.

After I Died

It was a big surprise, I tell you now.
After the dreading and threading of it
through the cloth of living for so long.
And no comfort in the friend who says:
'It's just like sleep—you won't even *know*
you're dead'. Well, excuse me, but I dream
profusely and I like those credible dreams.
They are still 'me', and without them and
the waking up again part, it isn't just sleep.
It's nothingness, while the worms and beetles
nibble and gnaw their random tunnels
through you. Anyway, it was a big surprise.
A vast hotel of marble pillars
and all these sweeping staircases,
only kind of ethereal, not really marble.
There were no porters,
so I had to carry my own bags.
At the reception desk I was afraid
to bring up the 'H' words,
being unsure exactly where I was.
But the receptionist, young and pleasant,
was obviously used to the stunned,
worried look and said softly:
'You're just here—and there's no name for it.'

'Will I see other people I know?' I asked.
She handed me a beige card with two instructions:
Please construct your afterlife according to
your personal preference.
In doing this, do not use any preconceptions
from religion or Hollywood.
'You mean I have to make it up myself?' I asked.
She nodded, and her uniform turned beige as well.
'Have the others thought of anything original?'

I persisted, feeling a bit annoyed.
There was a whiff of brimstone in the foyer.
She glanced around quickly and leaned forward.
Her eyes brimmed with compassion,
like Gene Tierney in *The Ghost and Mrs Muir.*
'No one has yet—not on my shift.
But you can stay here and think about it,
or you can take one of those staircases to a room.
But remember, that's not what they are.
It's just the best you could do.'

Poetry at Hanging Rock

At 8.30 a.m. the shiny convoy stretches
around two suburban blocks:
a slow queue of lumbering 4WDS
deposits girls at the private school.

There is a train station twenty metres away,
brightly painted, beckoning hopefully,
but still the behemoths come, bearing fruit
of the merchant and managerial class.

With shrill cries of daily recognition
the girls fall into extravagant embraces.
Their mothers drive away for work
or the gym, or for days unguessable.

One morning a new, golden child alights
from the back of a coach and four.
Small wings sprout from her back,
and the stained-glass chapel windows
scramble like a kaleidoscope.

Wordlessly she leads the senior class,
two by two, past the small park
where bony settlers are buried,
to a rocky outcrop at the river bend.

Thirty straw-hatted Mirandas,
lit by the glow of their mobile phones.
By the granite there is honeysuckle
escaped from a garden.

They linger here a while, as if held
by something half-remembered:
a young boatman who stands watching
the tide with his sleeves rolled up.

Then all turn back, chattering again.
None seems magically transformed,
none swallowed by the dark rocks.
They return as if from geology class.

But that term there are thirty stories
submitted in English class about a witch
or angel figure with daring wings,
and unasked for, mysterious dreams.

The Headmistress inserts a tart editorial
in the school newsletter about the sin
of unoriginality, and a reminder that dreams
are but the smoke of a life burned away.

Then for no reason she writes in her diary:
all that summer day I waited,
the flowers each spoke their name,
and I was open as the clover's honey,
but my other half never came.

The Lie of Biology

At Southampton my Great Aunt Eastman
shows me the table where every Christmas
she wrapped a Rover or Tiger annual
filled with soccer stories and Spitfires,
bound for steamy, respectful Brisbane.
In the photo I have a Dennis Lillie moustache,
like every Australian male in England, 1975.

In Scotland I travel through Perthshire,
Grandma Morris's town of Blairgowrie.
There are burly townsfolk in singlets
scattered along the steps by the river,
sunning themselves under a July sky.
In the photo I am wearing a padded jacket
designed for mountain snow survival.

Striding through Freiburg in August
I feel the Rhine in my blood, the pine song.
Then I discover great grandfather Berndt
came from northern Koenigsberg,
home of the Prussian officer class
and the meticulous, obedient bureaucrat.
In the photo I am the long-haired
conscientious objector with blue eyes.

Great grandfather Nilsson left Bergen
in 1874 for the Windjammers and tropical
Queensland. I am delaying this fourth
and final trip, the one to Norway.
I can see the photo already. There I am,
standing by multi-coloured boats glistening
with rain, or on the edge of a fiord
with a beanie pulled down over my ears,
looking genetically uncomfortable,
trying to smile my way into the frame.

The Romance of the Clockmakers

In 1675 Charlotte of Paris,
beautiful, wealthy, aspiring inventor,
advertised for a husband to be.
Each should bring a timepiece and by this test
she would choose the suitor
whose clock pleased her best.

So with their intricate machines they came.
A Swiss unwrapped a watch that kept
perfect time he proudly claimed.
Sulkily unadorned and unfussed,
of spare Calvinistic design,
its owner boasted of his disgust
at ornament or engraving.
His worn woollen trousers proved
his sincerity and savings.

At her window she released a dove
and saw Herr Wolf below arriving
in German brocade vest and glove.
But his watch was a skull manic;
a silver reminder that every moment
brings us closer to the Great Mechanic.
'The *memento mori* is an ugly trick'
she told him, wincing at its smile.
She sent him off with a finger click.

In winter, Charlotte's windows locked,
Christiaan Huygens of the Netherlands
came trudging with his pendulum clock.
She gaped as the brassy pendulum bold
ceaselessly swung back and forth,
then begged him to make her one in gold.
Excited Christiaan rubbed his hands,

explained the crucial oscillation
had been Galileo's plan.

'A mere copyist? You *steal* from your brothers?'
Her scowl grew fierce. He argued that science
must always build on the work of others.
'One ploughs, and another plants the flax.'
She sat and scowled. He cleared his throat.
'But I, of course, saw what it lacked.
I have here sketches for a spiral spring.
This will control the balance wheel.
I alone saw the future of this thing!'

She saw him anew with melting eye
felt faint, as if with running in a field
where potently scented poppies lie.
'A spiral spring?' she said with a flutter,
and brushed the dandruff from his lapel
with a hand as pale and soft as butter.

The hall was adorned, as was the carriage
with hundreds of golden keys and chimes;
Christiaan ventured a toast at their marriage:
'To the cogs that join, to the cuckoo revealed,
like a bridegroom's pressing passion'. As they
drove away at 3.00 pm the church bells pealed.
Charlotte relished the certainty of measure,
freed from the sun's uneven passage,
the autumnal loss of Nature's treasures.
The coach sprang and sped on polished wheels,
dashed from cobbles to country lanes,
past peasants at work in the shrinking fields.

Workplace Bullying

The legal secretaries are gloating in the corridor.
One of the solicitors—the new one—
is being shouted at because she didn't notice
that the senior partner's mail was put
in her tray by mistake. One of the secretaries
informed on her. Pettiness swells to the ceiling.
The secretaries fawn on the senior partner:
*Oh, Stephen, as if you don't have enough work
to do already, without this sort of thing.*
A thousand hornets hum around the photocopier.
Yesterday another solicitor was carpeted
by one partner for not completing a settlement
that another partner had said was not ready.
*You just don't listen, do you? You better
shape up and quickly.* Excuses can't
be made, excuses are just soft, toffee mud
for the hornets to build more towers with.
There is no appeal against the jibes,
the inconsistency, the poison of adrenalin.
Complain and you are described as 'difficult'.
The legal secretaries simper sweetly
outside the new solicitor's door:
would you like something from the coffee shop?
She smells it—it circulates like blood,
the perfume of fear that breeds excitement.
She knows the tiny barbs can't be touched
without spreading under the skin, or sticking
to the fingers, like a chocolate éclair.

Biggles Flies Again at 95

Head for that clearing in the jungle Captain Bigglesworth—
a bumpy landing and a wink from Ginger.

Jump out nimbly as possible,
spray machine gun fire at surrounding bushes
where gullible natives in the pay of the Hun
could be lurking to ambush a chap.

But you've landed in the London botanic gardens,
killed seventeen French tourists
and a Bulgarian nanny pushing a pram.

The frogs won't be missed, nor the commie.
Setting up HQ in a greenhouse, you wait for orders,
which anachronistically come in a telegram
from swarthy, foreign types in Brussels.

'Age of heroic individual never existed. Stop.
If you had been better at Latin and History
than rugby, you might have understood that. Stop.
Shake hands firmly with Ginger. Stop.
Place pistol in mouth—think (if possible)
of European Union. Stop. Pull trigger. Stop.'

Harry Potter Book 8

Harry is now at Hogwarts University.
He enrols in creative writing, but all his
stories and poems have the same theme:
the eventual discovery that good and evil
may be interdependent constructs.
The lecturer tells him his work is derivative.

This brings us to chapter ten where
Voldemort makes a final comeback.
He infiltrates the university by reshaping
himself as a chocolate dispensing machine.
Half the first years are sucked through
the coin slot into his toxic stomach.
Harry does an *emeticus* spell in rhyming couplets.
The weeping first years are retrieved,
though partly digested and hard to recognise.

Meanwhile, Hermione's work for house elf rights
wins her the Nobel Peace Prize.
But she is unlucky in love.
Boys find her intellect threatening.
She experiments with going out with older men,
but finds them all sad and needy.
At Cambridge she joins a rock/techno girl band
called Virginia Werewolf.
The band wins five Aria awards.
Rita Skeeter writes it up for the Murdoch press
with the headline 'Witch Bitch Gets Rich.'

Harry becomes headmaster of Hogwarts School.
There is a noisy protest staged by
fundamentalist Christians from Idaho.
But nothing scary stalks the musty corridors

except prefects, privilege and nostalgia.
Voldemort and Dumbledore enter the same
wizard retirement village.
There the old adversaries sit
side by side in their striped deck chairs,
warmed by Phoenix fires.
Unicorns herd below like small clouds.
They both grumble about the younger generation,
their selfishness in putting work-life balance
before vocation.

And Harry, now middle-aged, paunchy,
two novels published to mixed reviews,
takes to visiting the magic wood each night,
walking marathon, thoughtful miles like Dickens.
The wood seems smaller than in his childhood,
and dark shapes follow him everywhere.
He thinks of slowing so they can draw closer,
to see if he recognises anything in their faces.
He considers never going home to Ginny or the kids.
Just staying here
where there is always more to wonder at
than to forget or justify.

Roy Orbison in Germany

A life-sized Roy Orbison statue in Houston
distils a single drop of water from the left eye
on each anniversary of his birth. A tiny bead
trickles from behind the wax sunglasses.
My Munich taxi driver has read this somewhere.
*Only the Americans could be so gullible
and show also such little respect* he says.

He asks me my favourite Orbison song.
He has a PhD in Norse sagas and his wife
has just left him. My girlfriend has phoned
asking for time out from our relationship
to see someone else. It's a lot of new information
to process. At midnight we are headed
for a castle an hour away in the country,
because all the hotels are full for a convention.
The castle will be expensive and festooned
with the small heads of horned creatures.

I decide it is not 'Pretty Woman' but 'Only the Lonely'.
*Ah, says the driver, but—Nur den Einsamer—
in German you lose both the rhythm and rhyme.*
The Autobahn sucks us into black night.
We sing in English, the driver a third above.
It feels very good, so we sing 'Blue Bayou'
and a couple more. He turns off the meter.
*Such a plain, shy man, he says—but that voice.
When I was young I thought Mozart's requiem
said it all.* I did too. We drive on in silence,
sure that Roy knows the way we feel tonight,
though probably not if she's coming back to me.

Academic Party

At the party an elegant new lecturer from France says
I'm tired of men who want to suck on
my breasts like limpets. I just want someone to cook
me a meal, fuck me and go home.
The other women laugh and nod.
I am the only man in this group.
Behind me someone is telling
the Dean about his plans to double
the number of research grants in three years.
They move off together.
A history lecturer hands me a glass of wine.
We've rated all the men in the department here tonight,
she says—what they'd be like in bed.
We reckon Henderson would carefully fold his clothes
after taking them off.
Henderson passes by the group
and I see him adjust his tie.
Well, as long as I wasn't rated bottom! I think
of saying with a light comic touch, but wisely say nothing.
They swim in an ocean of male insecurity.
You better look out for Professor Arnold one woman says
to the new lecturer—*he expects constant flattery*
since his bloody book won that American prize.
The French lecturer opens her eyes wide.
Then I will be sure to constantly flatten him she says.
We all chuckle at the Gallic word-play.
Drawn by the merriment, two other men join our group
and turn the topic of conversation
to whom is likely to be promoted this year.
No longer a guest in another world,
I go outside and, non-drinker, non-aligned,
pour my wine into a pot plant.

In Search of Shakespeare

A riddle still the life of Master Shakespeare.
Biographers pad books with weasel words:
'may well haves', 'likely dids' and 'it would seems'.
Unlike all others of his time and tier.

Not one small scrap of paper, not one gloss,
marries him with the muse. None paused to mourn
his death in verse, as they did for Bacon, Sidney,
Jonson, Marlowe. No one gave a toss.

The documents we do have tell us what?
He bought up plays, commodities and land,
kept company with criminals and whores,
lent money, and sued his debtors for the lot.

Quick to prosecute and alarm,
an entrepreneur, market economy man,
risen to wealth, his father bought
a phoney coat of arms.

Neglected to educate his daughters,
or visit his wife for eleven years.
Left no books in his will, before
a nameless grave by Avon's waters.

Then must I see him at eventide,
after locking up his money drawers,
sit deliberately at his desk
and reaching into his sensitive side,

or left half of brain, conjuring from somewhere,
aristocratic knowledge of French, the Law,
Court manners and intrigues, to write sublime
of evil usury (a bit hypocritical there),

putting aside his love of real estate
for tenderer musings and sighings—
the tricks of nymphs and shepherds,
the profit and loss a heart creates.

Practising Blues Piano Scales

The trick is not to think too hard
I tell myself.
These scales were made from
lynchings in plain daylight,
Methodist hymns and melancholy,
love in hard times.
For a few notes maybe I'm there,
then a spoiled child wails
in our neighbour's house
because a toy has fallen over.
I'm back with nothing worth lamenting,
except everything.
It should be saved for someone
with a lowdown achin' heart disease,
or someone caught in the headlights
and running through the trees.

Lewis Carroll's Counsellor

And so, reverend, when you took
those photos of young girls,
you thought you were preserving
a memory of innocence, is that right?
The waif who engenders pity?

No, you're not invisible behind the cushions.
And I don't want to hear what Alice thinks,
that's just your way of making this into
something you can control. Do you see that?
You grew up in the Victorian age—deal with it.

Yes, I know it's become a classic,
but the tabloids wouldn't care about that.
You remember what we said about boundaries?
I'm sure the White Rabbit would agree.

Very well, I'll see you again next week.
Keep doing the calculus and algebra—
no harm in that. Give your lectures,
and photograph the squirrels
in your back yard. Good afternoon.

Mrs Harris, could you please send Mr Barrie in?
Oh, and if he's wearing that pirate hat again,
do ask him to take it off.

George Bush in Brisbane

I'm sure I see him, the jaunty smile
of a man who knows more than he
can let on, driving his pick-up truck
down Queen Street. Same hair, same eyes,
same hand-tooled belt with the silver buckle.
It makes no sense, because this is Brisbane
and George has to be in Washington being
briefed by Dick Cheney, or in Texas, being
buoyed by Laura, the perky ex-school teacher.
And where are all the security guys?
But at the lights I say 'Hi, George',
just to test it out, and he, a bit sheepish,
says 'Hi' right back, and before the light
changes, 'Y'all doin' a mighty fine job'.
On his back window are stickers saying
'Freedom' and 'Jesus loves you',
in red, white and blue. I walk around
the shops, digesting it all, and decide
something has happened, something big.
But that night, while I'm worrying,
the Prime Minister comes on TV,
saying 'nothing happened today'
and I feel better, like I still fit
in my own country. I guess.

Breaking Up

Whenever I broke up with a girlfriend
my best friends would take me on a picnic,
somewhere an hour inland from Brisbane,
through bleached pastures to a neutral creek.

Sitting in the back of the car, I would explain
the signs I had seen coming, her faults, for I was
practised in alchemy, turning sweet to bitter.
Even heartbreak has its wits, its vanity.

Each time I became an explorer in a new world,
sunlight on river gums more intense than usual,
though harder to translate. And above, the cold air
of an invisible galaxy, leaving a thirst for stars.

The streetlights would guide us back in silence
while I engineered a heart transplant,
metal clips on the arteries, operating quickly,
her cards and photos gathered in a plastic bag.

Tragically though, it was always endurable.
Only heroes and beggars die from love affairs.
After the etiquette of pain and the recovery room,
gloves snapped off, a stray strand of her hair.

Pets

I just don't get it with people and their pets.
The money we spend on pet food
could feed the world's poor.
Cats carry fatal diseases and spread faeces
over their fur with their own saliva.
Dogs remove the faces from children
and are then described in the news as 'family pets'.
'It was out of character' the owner says, puzzled
that a wolf descendant should act this way.

Of course, one accepts that a pet can be
a non-argumentative, second-best kind
of companion for the elderly.

Actually, I feel sorry for them,
neurotically yipping and barking
from yard to yard along our street:
'this is my place', 'this is my place',
or 'you belong to me — don't leave.'
A frenzy of possessiveness,
tiny trumpets of despair.

Les A. Murray versus John Tranter at the Sydney Cricket Ground

It's a capacity crowd for today's Poetry Cup Final
and a colourful sight they make.
At the centre of the oval the poets shake hands
and the umpires take up their positions.

Les won the toss, so he occupies the crease
and Tranter runs in with some nasty non-referential similes:
'She has a smile like Sydney Harbour. Her new boyfriend
is like a swimming pool with a headache, or adultery in Borneo'.

Murray forward defends with a country afternoon:
there's a fete on, brown-armed mothers in white aprons
smooth their hair back from honest foreheads
and hum quietly to themselves
as they lay out strawberry jam and cream.

Tranter sneers, and tosses up
five hundred cheerleaders and a New York rock band.
Their wicked smiles and soaring riffs
have the crowd clapping in unison.
The young women blow kisses like Doris Day.

Murray twirls his bat, strokes through the covers
and it's a family barbeque. Then he cuts savagely past point
for the big one: it's five hundred milk cows,
their eyelashes catching the golden twilight
that trickles down gullies. They call softly to each other
with the simple wisdom of their race.
Their flanks are like velvet. As night falls
in the distance, a lone harmonica plays.

The crowd begins to feel ashamed —
they look at one another in confusion.
But from a longer run up, Tranter bangs in a bouncer

and the crowd holds its breath:
a crazy squadron of Sabre jets circles the Ground:
the pilots are karate experts with broken hearts—
their engines run on perfume and neurotic dreams.
'A second chance,' they moan, 'I want to grow young!'
Their intentions growl like the monster from a 50s movie,
then the monster is you, and it's 2.00 a.m.
with the kids in bed, a police siren in the distance,
and the au pair asleep with her head in your lap . . .

Murray staggers backwards and the crowd gasps—
can Les be weakening? He closes his eyes
and extends his arms, Christ-like.
Suddenly there is the smell of wattle and Sunday baking—
Mum's starched apron and the promise of ponies,
dew on the paddock,
children laughing under the peppermint trees.
They hear Dad's voice calling from the veranda—
and Mum's singing now,
in the time of holiday, and stories by the fire.

The crowd all start to cry. They're crying in public,
and within themselves. Big pie-stained tears.
They're embracing one another
when Tranter shouts 'Foul! Image tampering!'
The umpires confer and fidget with their counters.
Tranter strides down the pitch—but Murray pivots,
tackles him head-on and they crash to the ground.
Murray goes for the North Coast head-lock, but Tranter
does a Singapore twist and rolls free.

The crowd looks up and the sky is filled with angels.
There are golden ones in singlets and shorts, swinging axes,
and scarlet ones packing Lugers and French dictionaries.

They hurl themselves at one another time and again,
delicate pieces break from wings and flutter to the grass.
The crowd is silent.
A small dog faints.
Play is abandoned due to bad light.

Blaming Your Childhood

I'm sick of you all complaining
about your childhood problems.
Blaming your mother for your
poor choice of wife,
your father for the remoteness
of your children.

Most of us here had it pretty good,
whether there was a nasty divorce
or an over-protective parent.
Take a look at Africa and spare me
your small sufferings.

Outside there is a jack-knife night
and a war that does not know you.
Memorise your address,
touch your unbroken face.

Sit at random bus stops.
Unlike the escapee, you can
answer the ticket collector
in your own language.

Like Candide, cultivate your garden
not your grudges.
Walk over the crooked bridge
to et cetera and to so on.

Hold the Grave Close

Glimpse the young woman
through the window
of the railway station.
Her perfume devours you.
She hurries into sunlight,
her bronze hair like fruit.
Where she is going does not matter,
only the sparkle of afternoon,
the buzz of a fly.

You think she was wearing blue.
A single chord from a piano
followed her down the path.

Thirty years later
the window still dazzles with geraniums,
a balloon rolls across the platform.
Someone steps into the sparkle of afternoon,
her golden hair like fruit.
Her perfume devours you.

∽

The philosophers fumble their shoes,
their pillows crackle like paper.

All that matters now is the geranium window
and her warm throat.

Feel your chest rise in the crisp air,
trace the veins on the back of your hand.
Hold the grave close.

Metamorphosis

A beetle woke up one morning
to find it had become Franz Kafka.
There were many challenging issues.
It had no literary background,
so its books came slowly.
It was stuck with a tedious
public service job.
An angry fiancée turned up
and demanded it marry her
without further delay.
The beetle felt no attraction to her
but could not explain why.
How it yearned for its
former life, free amongst
the silky flowers
and fragrant leaves.
The beetle's journals
in their scratchy scrawl
were dark with pessimism
and thoughts of suicide.
What is the point of books
it kept asking. What is the point.
In the end they will
only be consumed
by insects.

Notes to the Poems

Crusoe Revisited: Alexander Selkirk (1676–1721) was a Scottish sailor who spent four years as a castaway. It is generally thought his story was a model for Defoe's Crusoe. By the time Selkirk was rescued, because he had not spoken for so long and also forgotten some vocabulary, his rescuers found it difficult to understand him. Selkirk never adjusted to civilization. He returned to Scotland a rich man from the capture of a Spanish ship, but he made his home in a cave where he lived a reclusive life for the next fifteen years. Aged forty-five he returned to the sea, but died after drinking infected water.

Northern Hairy Nosed Wombat: This animal survives only in a six square mile site, now fenced to keep out cattle and sheep, within a small national park near Epping Forest Station in central Queensland. It is likely to become extinct if threats continue, as it is Australia's most critically endangered mammal.

Jim Corbett Has the Idea for a National Park: Jim Corbett (1875–1955) was famous worldwide as a reluctant hunter of tigers who had become 'man-eaters'. A small number of tigers killed hundreds of women and men and terrorised regions where the hill folk of Kumaon and Garhwal lived. But Corbett was also a pioneer conservationist and in later life turned entirely to the camera. A national park and tiger reserve in India is now named after him, as is one of the five remaining subspecies of tigers, *panthera tigris corbetti*. His books have been reissued recently by Oxford University Press.

Koreelah Ranges, Northern NSW: For over twenty years I was part of a cooperative of six environmentally-minded people who owned a thousand acres and a cabin at the junction of the Clarence River and Tooloom Creek in the Koreelah Ranges of northern New South Wales and who had it declared a state nature reserve. In 2006 we sold it to the NSW National Parks, in the hope that the remnant dry rainforest and wildlife, including platypus (hence the name 'Platypus Flat'), rock wallabies and rich birdlife will continue to be protected.

Anatomy of a Forest: 'Those who see all creatures in themselves/And themselves in all creatures know no fear'. *The Upanishads*.

The Man Who Couldn't See Colours: Based on an experience of a meditation centre.

Recording the Birds: Helen Horton, OAM, has been an influential conservationist and writer in Queensland. Her painstaking field recordings of birds are available on CDs from the Australian Broadcasting Corporation.

Under the Cover of Shared Pleasures: These words came as part of an email from John Kinsella in a different context. I decided to use them as the first line and random starting point of a poem.

Carbon Dioxide: Joseph Priestley (1733–1804) was a dissenting minister (the reason for his rejection from Cook's voyage), an abolitionist and a supporter of the American and French revolutions. During his research into the properties of gases he advanced knowledge of oxygen and photosynthesis, observing that plants repaired 'injured' air.

Taking Off from Cyprus: My father joined the RAAF when he turned 18 in 1942 and served as a pilot in the RAF, ultimately flying Beaufighters in the UK, Cyprus and Ceylon, as it then was.

Tavistock Square July 7, 2005: My wife and I were staying in a University of London flat in Tavistock Square through July, 2005.

Do We Have to Read the Set Books?: A poem arising from the curious aversion of some creative writing students to reading—though almost all aim to publish books themselves. I am indebted to Tom Wayman's poem, 'Did I Miss Anything?'

Six Curses: Inspired by Vicki Raymond's 'The Sending of Five' in her brilliant 1989 poetry collection *Small Arm Practice*.

Poetry at Hanging Rock: While the allusion is to Joan Lyndsay's novel, the poem is based geographically on a prominent Anglican girl's school near the Brisbane River. The rest is imagined. However, well after the poem was finished, including the last stanza, I found this quotation from the Headmistress of 1929–1947: 'The greatest joys in life come to those ... who with stars in their eyes ... creep step by step nearer their heart's desire.'

The Romance of the Clockmakers: This poem draws on the history of particular clocks and their inventors, though Charlotte is of course fictional.

Roy Orbison in Germany: Based on an experience during a visit to Germany's south in 1990.

In Search of Shakespeare: Though it is still heresy to say so, there remain questions about the Shakespeare authorship issue that have not yet been answered entirely convincingly by the Stratfordians. Diana Price's *Shakespeare's Unorthodox Biography* and Patrick Buckridge's articles provided material for this poem.

Les A Murray versus John Tranter at the Sydney Cricket Ground:
Les Murray and John Tranter often have been seen as the unofficial leaders of rival schools of Australian poetry.